# Walking In The
# Shadows Of Death

First published in Great Britain in 2015

# Walking In The Shadows Of Death

Roy Merchant

I dedicate this book to all those members of the family, friends and work colleagues who, when there was no more light,
Prayed for me.

# Contents

# Foreword

Life is a journey. A never-ending, running war between hope and hopelessness.

Because life must end in death, hope seldom wins.

However, it fights some magnificent and noble battles and every now and then, hope is victorious.

These thoughts and story reflect the part I played and continue to play in one of those battles.

It is not over yet!

# Acknowledgments

The poem "Stay Focused" was inspired by the work "Desiderata" and acknowledgement is given.

# Prelude

I was born in the Blue Mountains of Jamaica, halfway up the John Crow Mountain, somewhere between Fellowship and Coopers Hill in a small village of some three hundred people called Brookdale in the parish of Portland.

Quite why it was called Brookdale was always an ironic mystery to me, as I never found a brook, not a proper brook anyway, and as for the dale, that had disappeared along with the brook, I suppose, a long, long time ago.

The local name for our village was also ironic. It was called Hambrooks and, being a village of Seventh Day Adventists who saw pork as unclean meat, calling the village Hambrooks was interesting.

We grew up as God-fearing Christians who trusted God in every part of our lives. He – yes, it was HE – looked after us through the week, kept us away from the devil and brought us all to Church on Saturdays, where we worshipped him all day.

He would always protect us from evil, even if we had to walk through the valley of the shadows of death. This had a profound effect on all of us Christians, as we always knew that in the end everything would be OK, and if it was not OK then it was not yet the end.

This faith allowed us to move mountains without fear and ensured that we always had a positive outlook on our lives. We knew we could trust in the Lord and it would all be OK. This outlook kept a smile on our faces most of the time. The smile also kept us happy. In many ways, I was just a simple Jamaican country boy.

I came to England in the cold grey winter of 1961 and although the journey and its subsequent consequences had dampened my positivity and blind faith in God, there was still a sense that everything would be fine if I trusted him a little more. And it was fine for a long while.

I joined the Navy, spent some time in submarines and three of my naval years in the bars, shanty towns and docks of Singapore, Hong Kong, Subic Bay, Colombo in Ceylon, before it became Sri Lanka, and Bombay, before it became Mumbai, in India.

I left the Navy and became an electronics engineer, just when colour television exploded onto the English market and everyone could afford to rent one.

I went into management and at thirty-five was a manager of six television and VHS rental shops in north London.

As televisions became more reliable, customers started buying them more and more until the rental market died. By then I had left and gone into Local Government, where by God's grace, my positive outlook and naval discipline I found some success as a resource manager.

At fifty-one I was a senior resource manager reporting to the director and looking to build a team around me as preparation for the next director's vacancy.

Then the heart problems started.

The two poems that follow in the prelude reflect the way I saw the world before my heart failed. It was a philosophy based on the abundance principles, on how best to live your life and how life progresses. Now, I am not so sure about it.

# Life

**I first met him on the day he was born.**
He was lying down… just having a rest
Gently… trying to focus on the dewy morn
His only means of survival… his mother's breast.

His mother looked on in wonderment
Afraid to touch this fragile gift
The child looked on in wonderment
Afraid to leave this rocklike gift.

Bonds that last for eternity
Instantaneously coming to being
First days going by like infinity
First of many days child will be seeing.

I looked at him again when he was two years old
So confident that he was in control
Running now… jumping now… talking… endlessly bold
Future just something that will unfold.

Bright eyes beaming…
Cheeks so gleaming…
Eyes just streaming endlessly.
Fine teeth showing…
No tears flowing…
His childhood growing relentlessly.

I glimpsed him fleetingly by a lake
I guessed he was no more than five
He looked at me as if there was a mistake

He knew for the first time that he was alive.

Thrusting now... demanding now
The world was his... and his alone
Fighting here... delighting there
Sitting on daddy's shoulders... all the way home.

Bright eyes beaming...
Cheeks so gleaming...
Eyes just streaming endlessly.
Fine teeth showing...
No tears flowing...
His childhood growing relentlessly.

At sixteen he was a handsome young man
Listening to nothing but his own voice
The meaning of life... the yin and the yang
Were too simple to ruffle his elegant poise.

I met him again at twenty-five
The first day of the rest of his life
Full of himself and a little naive
Confidence brimming... sharp as a knife.

Contact lens beaming...
Hard cheeks gleaming...
Eyes just roving endlessly.
A capped tooth showing...
A few tears flowing...
His childhood dying relentlessly.

It was seven long years till I saw him again
Up to his eyeballs in nappies and pins
House rent and rate... baby irate... still numb from lifelong pains
His world just going into an infinite spin.

Money was now his Godlike model
His strategy for survival... just a little askew
His hopes and dreams... in a warren-like muddle
No clear future... just a frightening view.

Spectacled eyes dreaming...
Sallow cheeks steaming...
Aches and pains hurting endlessly.
False teeth showing...
Grey hairs flowing...
His middle years dying relentlessly.
His children missing...
His lifestyle ending...
His heart just aching endlessly.
New clothes not coming...
Money... just going
Reality just hitting him relentlessly.

"Why the pain... why the long road of sorrow...?
Is my life not worth any bends...?
Oh...! For a life of one sweet tomorrow...
Where loneliness isn't my only friend..."

Spectacled eyes not seeing...
Gristled cheeks convening...
Grandchildren growing endlessly.
False teeth not fitting...
The toupee no longer sitting...
Coming to terms reluctantly.
New friendships beginning...
Mind... no longer spinning...
Years going by relentlessly.
Stairs... getting higher...
Exertions... getting rarer...
Some good friends dying unexpectedly.
Armchair... so inviting...
Sleep is so exciting...
Seeing family more frequently.

He was looking in the mirror
In one of his eightieth years
When he recognised me
As what he was trying to find
We held each other...
And we shed a few tears
I... the long lost...
Forgotten friend...
**Was his peace of mind.**

Epilogue.
I was with him on the day that he died
He was lying down just having a rest
Desperately… trying to focus on life… as it's implied
And gently falling… back… into Mother Nature's breast.
In the end he smiled and said he felt a little odd
**Then finally gave himself to God.**

# Stay Focussed

**Remember to:**
Stay focussed in the middle of the noise and bustle
And remember the peace and tranquillity of silence.
While you are strong... there are occasions when being
Seen as being weak and fragile is the best line to take.
You don't have to wait until you are loved before you love.

Speak your truth quietly and clearly...
But listen... listen to all information
For sometimes the wisest words...
Are spoken by the biggest fools
And everyone has an important story to tell.

Walk away from the rudeness of aggressive people
Once you have heard what they have to say
Staying and returning their aggression...
Makes you worse than they...
For you know better.

Do not compare yourself with anyone else...
For this will either make you vain or bitter
For always there will be greater and...
Lesser achievements than yours...
Take pride in what you do...
And what you achieve...

Remember...
Dreams are reality awaiting their time

Stay focussed… on your dreams…
For they are tomorrow's reality
Pursue your career…
It is an important part of the baton
In the relay race of life.

Trust everyone until they prove…
They cannot be trusted.
This may be painful now and then
But in the long run of time…
You will find that people
Are virtuous… caring… loving…
Protective… heroic… giving…
And trustworthy.

Be yourself…
Evolve and grow…
Mature like wine…
But do not change
See the world… understand its strengths and weaknesses
But maintain and love your own sense of self at all times.

Listen well to the words of the wise
You will find that the years of life…
Seeing and observing… have made the elders…
Arrive closer to some fundamental truths…
Some of them may appear as if they will not know…
But listen… before dismissing them as fakes.
They may surprise you.

Keep your mind… your body… and your soul…
Clean… healthy… and as pure as life will allow.
But do not become obsessed with this…
Remember… the ultimate enjoyment in life
Is when it all balances…

Do not seek loneliness for a friend
But do not run away from the medicinal qualities…
Of solitude.
Be gentle with yourself
In a disciplined way
Forgetting not that you…
Are a child of the Universe
No greater than the atom
No less than the stars
You were destined to be here
Time and space is unfolding
Exactly as it is meant to do.

Be in harmony with your god…
Be it nature or Jehovah…
Whatever you decide it to be.
And remember…
In the confusion of pursuing your dreams
Be at peace with yourself.
For with all its politics…
Pain… lies… deceit… wrongs…
And broken dreams…
It is still a beautiful world.
**Stay focussed.**

# Book 1

# A Short But True Story

# Walking In the Shadows of Death

The pain was not that intense. It was not a pain that I felt had the strength and power to kill me. No, to me, it felt more like a gentle prod. Like someone jabbing me with a piece of wood, when mentally, I was far away and certainly not ready. I knew something had happened, but I was not sure what.

We do not prepare ourselves for the first heart attack or heart failure. It comes like one of the horsemen of the apocalypse, whether we are ready for him or not. I was not ready.

Even now, when I look back, I am not sure whether it was a heart attack or not; like cancer patients, we feel that it is too serious to be accepted as part of our past and future, so we deny it.

I can now look back and pretend that just maybe I was suffering from stress and overwork. The pain was not that intense. It was not, I imagine, like a mother giving birth. I knew there was something wrong; I hoped it was not my heart because I only had one and it is all so final if it stopped working. It was not as if I could retrain another limb or organ to do its work, or ask my lungs to carry out the function of my now departed friend. It... is... so... Final.

Yes, I should have known that my lifestyle would bring me to this moment of reckoning. All my family had been telling me to slow down and relax a bit. A week or so before the event I was not sleeping very well and getting by with just four hours' sleep every night. Work was chaotic. I was now managing another service as well as my own. That represented another sixty people and increased budget responsibilities of another £13 million per annum. The new service was failing, with all sorts of people, systems and finance problems to solve. There was pressure from the community and from the executive board to sort it out very quickly, before the papers got hold of it and made it even more difficult to improve.

However, I felt that I was a master of the universe and I could continue at the fast pace a lot longer. Besides at fifty-one, I was still physically fit and strong. So what if the doctor had said my blood pressure was high? A lot of people had high blood pressure. That just goes with the lifestyle I was leading. Funny, even now I am not convinced that my lifestyle had anything to do with it. It may have been just a genetic aberration.

I had just finished mowing the lawn. The lawn was 100ft by 40ft. I had trimmed the edges with the trimmer and mowed it in a record fifteen minutes and was hurtling up the stairs, when on the tenth rung, I felt a helicopter going off in my chest. It wasn't painful, just unusual. My heart was beating so fast it sounded as if it was humming. I shouted to Sue, my then partner, now my wife, to come and listen to it. She came and said "My goodness! You had better get some rest. You know, that sounds like your heart is playing up." I said, "Nah, don't be silly. It is just me doing the lawn in the sun, you watch. I'll just have that tea you were going to make and I will be as right as rain." And I was. After five or so minutes I was fine.

The day turned out to be a scorcher and, being Saturday, I had a lot to do. While Sue and the kids went gallivanting all over the shops of Ilford and Walthamstow, I had to do the serious business of putting together a specification for a computer system I intended to buy, and then go to the local business park to see if they had one and what the cost would be.

I rushed out of the cool car into the blazing sun and was going through the electronic turnstile, when I suddenly heard the helicopter going off in my chest again, only this time it was followed by nausea and dizziness. I grabbed hold of a handrail to keep myself upright then found a chair to sit on, until my senses came back to me.

It was at this stage, I began to wonder if there was something wrong. At first, I wondered whether I should head straight for the hospital, which was about five miles away, or head for home, which was three miles away. I decided that I would have a cold drink, make sure I was fine then drive home as slowly and carefully as I could. I got home safely, got an hour's nap and felt fine for the rest of the weekend.

It was the following Monday at 2.30pm when the next attack came and this convinced me there was something wrong and worse, it was not going to go away.

I was chairing a meeting between my management team and our parking services contractor in my office when the helicopter in my chest called again. This time it stayed for approximately five minutes, turned my fingers white as a sheet, and then left me as mysteriously as it came, breathless and confused. I felt now that there was something seriously wrong and I decided to go to the hospital immediately after I got home that evening. Something told me I was not going to be at work the next day, so quietly, I gave my secretary lots of things to do and asked her to cancel the meetings for the next day. When she asked why, I just said I would probably be away.

I got home, told Sue and she dropped me off at the King George's Hospital Accident and Emergency Service. The triage nurse took my pulse and my blood pressure and waltzed me straight through to get an ECG. This showed irregular heartbeats or, as I eventually came to understand it, ventricular tachycardia. My problem now had a name, not one I had ever heard before, but at least I knew I was not imagining it.

Ventricular tachycardia (VT) for the uninitiated is an arrhythmia or irregular heart rhythm that originates in the pumping chambers of the heart, or the ventricles. The normal heart beats at up to 100 beats per minute. With VT, the heart suddenly starts beating at anything up to 220 beats per minute. It occurs in people who have damaged ventricular chambers, acquired unfortunately as a by-product of a heart attack, or they pick up a myocardial infection. Scar tissue creates the environment where a local electrical circuit comes into being in the ventricle.

When activated, under certain specific circumstances, this can take over from the normal control circuits of the heart, leading to a rapid arrhythmia arising from a single area within the pumping chambers. Because the frequency is faster than the heart's natural electrical cycle, it takes over the heartbeat for the length of the arrhythmia. Again as the speed is so rapid, the heart is damaged and the rhythm does not follow the normal electrical pattern of the heart. The functionality of the heart reduces significantly, which again, as a by-product, also encourages low blood pressure.

The lack of oxygen in the blood, caused by the fast heart rhythm, causes shortness of breath, weakness, dizziness, light-headedness, and fainting. It also, sometimes, causes a feeling of fluttering (or helicopters going off as I remembered it) in the chest, heart conditions such as high blood pressure, poor blood supply to the heart muscle, tumours, and infections. Other medical ailments, such as thyroid disease, certain lung diseases, electrolyte imbalance, and alcohol and drug abuse, are also possible with the tachycardia. In its most extreme form, ventricular tachycardia can be fatal, as I was to find out. In some patients like me, it occurs even though there is no sign of infections or heart disease. This arrhythmia always requires treatment.

I was reading all this as I sat up in bed. I had been admitted to King George's Hospital Coronary Care Ward and I was not happy. I had so much work to do. I really thought all that would happen was that I would be told I had some murmur, given some tablets and sent home, where I would rest for a day or so then head back to the madhouse called work. I did not have an open-ended timeframe to spend in a hospital, whilst they searched for what could be like some Holy Grail.

I was told that they had seen the VT, but by the time they got round to treating it, it had disappeared and they could not treat it effectively if they could not see it. Being an electronics engineer by profession, I knew the frustrations and difficulties you encounter when trying to diagnose an intermittent fault, so when they said I had to stay in for a week, I did not complain.

During that week in May 2000, they tested my heart, my lungs, my blood, my urine, everything. They put me on the treadmill, they carried out a lung test and they found nothing.

On the Saturday, I packed my bags, put the prescription in my jacket, took a very close look at the spray they told me to spray under my tongue if I got any further chest pains and, with a sense of trepidation, foreboding and relief at going home, I went to the car, took the keys from Sue and we drove out of the hospital for what I thought would be the last time.

I took a further week away from work and on the following Monday, I headed for work and a morning of people genuinely extending their sorrow, pity, friendship and care to me. It was touching, because most of those people I had hardly got round to knowing on a personal basis. It was during this time also that, after thirteen years in the organisation, I finally began to realise that I had friends there and, even more important for a senior manager, who they were.

It did not take long for me to be introduced back to my in-tray, which was full, and my out-tray, which was empty. As a manager's role is to have them both empty, or if things are really bad to have the out-tray full and the in-tray empty, but never the other way round, I set to work.

Within a few days I was back to my old ways. In work at nine-thirty in the morning, home at nine-thirty in the evening, twenty-minute lunch of greasy sausage, bacon and chips, ten cigarettes in my lungs, stressful meetings with stressed-out staff and their belligerent union reps, dismissal hearings, Industrial Tribunals, chasing impossible deadlines and, oh yes, those quiet moments at seven o'clock in the evening when they have all gone home and you can think about how to deliver on that action or define that strategy that has eluded you all month. Ah yes, that was worth all the pain.

No time for exercise, no time for the children – they had been growing up without seeing me much anyway, apart from the school holidays, oh I always had the holidays. Quality time with the kids, I called it. I cringe with sadness when I look back at the love and experiences I sacrificed at the altar of ambition. What is worse, I can never get those days back and our relationship will always be different as a result of my obsession.

It was a quiet Sunday evening, the 26th November 2000, the last Sunday in November. Sue had prepared one of her special Sunday dinners and I had eaten too much of it. There was a quietness in the home as Ainsley, who was then coming up ten, and Sophie, coming up seven, started to get ready for school the next day.

Sue had just put Sophie in the bath and I was having a quiet word with Ainsley, when my old friend returned. He came out of the blue, only this time more ferocious than last May, when he came over that weekend. I knew what it was. I was not expecting him, but I remembered the signs he gave when he last made his presence felt.

This time as well as the helicopter going off, there was also a dull thud in my chest. In fact, it was the thud that made me realise what was going on. I got up and hoped that Ainsley did not see the concern in my face, went to the cupboard, where I kept the spray they had given me for moments such as this, and sprayed it under my tongue. There was a stinging painful sensation, which confirmed that I had a problem. I shouted to Sue that I thought she had better drop me off at the hospital. I did not need to say anything else. I guess both of us knew that there was unfinished business from last May. I mean nothing has ever finished so neatly in my life before. So why would it start now?

The ride to the hospital lasted no more than fifteen minutes. However, it was the start of a journey that would change my life forever and had I known what was to come, I am not sure I would have wanted to make the trip.

Back at King George's Hospital, I felt that the people in Accident and Emergency must know me personally by now; however, they see so many people daily that they cannot remember anyone. In to see the triage nurse; she took my blood pressure and pulse, called for a wheelchair and two nurses. I looked at Sue. Trepidation began to overtake me. Kids still played and missed the play-let completely. Into the diagnostic suite, ECG pads immediately strapped onto my chest, arms and legs. Machine switched on. Nurse smiled, called doctor, who came in to look.

Other nurses came wandering in to look at the printout, by then meandering its way down the ECG printer. Room cleared, transferred from bed to trolley, realised that I wouldn't be going home that night as I was wheeled to "Resus". Sue by now getting perturbed. Kids still played, not aware of what was unfolding. I was breathing very slowly and getting a bit concerned at the lack of information coming my way. Doctors crowded around like flies around faeces, and then disappeared again as it became obvious that no immediate drama was about to unfold. The heart monitor attached to me displayed the most horrendous-looking waveform I have ever seen in my life. It looked like something from hell. It was all spikes, long teeth, irregular, and looks nothing like what you would expect your beautiful, regular, romantic heart to produce. So this was what ventricular tachycardia looked like.

Another hour passed and soon it was 11.30pm; there was nothing else to be done, Sue took Ainsley and Sophie home. They had school the next day, Monday, and they would need their sleep. Kissed them all goodnight and gave Sue a squeeze on her way out. Still on a trolley in the A&E corridor. A nurse said I would be going up to Coronary Care Unit (CCU) soon. VT was still straddling my ECG machine like a colossus and I was breathing very slowly and methodically. Nurses fed me with different drugs from time to time throughout the night.

It was now 8.00am and I was still on the trolley in A&E. The porters decided that the bed was now ready for me in the Coronary

Care Unit and the nurse and porter took me up there. Sue came in at 10.00am. It was Monday, 27th November 2000.

Sue and I had some quiet times during the day as the doctors fought without success to control the VT. They ran through the list of likely drugs to control it, all without success, and by 3.00pm, they were pretty much out of ideas. Adrian, my oldest son, had arrived and he, Sue and I talked quietly; meanwhile, all around, the staff were busy, going from one patient to another, preparing some for surgery, some for discharge and some, alas, for the morgue.

By 4.30pm I was getting a supply of visitors in. Royston from work had taken the time to come and see me. Sue had just come back from picking up the children. Maxine, my sister, had just arrived. Other friends and relatives were milling around. The doctors were now getting a bit frantic trying to get the VT under control. They had been on the phone to Bart's Hospital, seeking their advice, and had also made arrangements to transfer me there later in the week. They kept coming back with different tablets, injections and drips to put into my body. Each one had no effect. The monstrous ECG monitor still looked down from its wall bracket ominously at us all.

I remember not being able to breathe. It was one of the drugs that created this feeling. I was there doing my slow breathing bit, while all around me doctors and nurses were running around trying to save my life, and then suddenly I was gone. Just like that. Adrian said I said quietly, just before I went, "That's it folks, I am out of here" and then I was silent and still, but I cannot recall that. I recall nothing.

I had always said that when it comes, let the four horsemen be quick, decisive and, beyond all, final. I do not want a long, drawn-out death, racked with pain like others I have seen. I do not want to know that I have six months to live, nor do I want time to make a will and plan my death, the way I see mothers prepare and plan for birth. I do not want to arrange the funeral, decide which suit and shoes to wear, or which hat shall be on my head. I would just want to die. When it comes.

I woke up covered in vomit. There was pandemonium everywhere; I saw people who I could not recall being at the hospital running up and down, saying things like "Sit still", as if I was going anywhere, and then I would drift back to sleep? I did not know how long these episodes were lasting. It was almost as if I were shifting in and out of reality, or realities. I did not know if I was sleeping. I was totally and absolutely overwhelmed by tiredness. There was a well of tiredness that I dipped into every time I was conscious again, which forced me back into sleep. I saw Sue and Adrian looking relieved. I saw Royston saying something or another to Adrian. Then I was off again.

That well of tiredness has stayed with me ever since. Each month it gets better, unless I am feeling particularly unwell or I have caught a virus, or something untoward has happened. I can track the improvements in my health, through this well of tiredness that has followed me since that day.

I finally woke up fully at 11.00pm, a full seven hours after my initial departure. Only Sue remained from the people who were there, keeping an eye on me. The nurses and doctors were checking charts, filling in their paperwork and giving out medicines. In the quiet of that moment, I heard:

"We nearly lost you," Sue said.
"What do you mean?" I replied.

She, quietly, in the dark, explained that at about 4.30pm, my heart stopped, probably due to a medicinal overload, that the crash team came and resuscitated me, that I was going in and out of consciousness for a long while. That she had been crying and the kids had been looking at her, not sure what was going on. That Adrian went grief stricken. That Royston was very helpful and reassuring during that dark moment. She said it was pandemonium, but eventually the Asian woman doctor managed to save my life and I had been awake since about 10.30pm, when she got back from dropping the kids round her mum's.

Love comes to you at quiet moments. It seldom comes at the peak of ecstasy or the loudness of parties. Nor does it often come when you are hurtling down the mountain slopes at a hundred miles per hour. It kinda creeps up on you, in the quiet moments. The moments you would probably forget, because they are unremarkable in themselves and only memorable because, when you look back, they made you realise something, so subtle, so life reaffirming that a totally different relationship springs out of that quiet moment.

That I loved Sue was never in doubt. How much I loved her, I did not know, but after that day, I knew how much she meant to me. It was not her beauty that in itself is remarkable enough. It is not her incessant, enchanting chatter. It is not the way she can and often does light up a room with her personality. It is simply her lightness of being. It is the gentleness she brings to our relationship. It is the stillness she has in her expression of love. It is the warmth she gives out without waiting to see if it is returned. It is the strength in her character. It is her refusal to accept anything but a positive outcome. We would spend a long time over the next few months getting to see each other at our best and our worst. In the end, I loved her more than I ever did before.

I looked up at the ECG monitor and for the first time in two days, I saw my old familiar friend sitting there, regular as clockwork.

The heartbeat and frequency were strong and consistent. I kissed Sue goodnight and drifted off to sleep, feeling confident about life for the first time in a long while.

Something woke me up; I did not, at first, realise what it was, just a tight shortness of breath, no helicopters, a squeezing of the chest muscles. I looked at the clock; it said 4.30am. As I came out of the deep sleep, a light started flashing at the control centre. I looked over there and they were looking back at me. I did not need to look at the monitor to know what was wrong. The VT had returned. I had gone off to sleep, thinking it was sorted, and that I would be home in a day or so, and now the very thing that had stopped my heart had returned.

The nurse ambled over, said hi, looked at the monitor as if she was manually confirming what was happening, and went back to make a phone call.

People started gathering round. That is when you know there is something wrong. You are all alone for hours then suddenly you find that there are people gathering, the way vultures do at the sign of death, the way flies seem to know that there is something interesting coming up.

The young Asian doctor came over and smiled at me; she was the one who had saved my life and I could see there was a genuine interest in my survival coming from her. She said to me that the VT had returned, that there was only one other medicine to try and if that did not work, they would have to take me down to the operating theatre to see if electric shock treatment to the heart would bring the normal heart rhythm back. She said she did not feel my body could hold out much longer and it was vital that whatever they did, they did quickly.

The young Asian nurse, who always seemed to be on duty, came over, looked and went away again. I think he was the one who went to wake Sue up.

Sue came over and I looked at her and for the first time in my life, I felt helpless. I had been the driving force behind all the things I had achieved in my life. I had started work at sixteen, Navy at seventeen, submarines at eighteen, and an electronics engineer at twenty-five and so on. Always in control, always ahead of the game, and here I was totally at the mercy of a greater force than myself. I did not know if I was going to live or die. From what they were saying, I had already died and had been given a second chance; how many more second chances did I have? It was at that moment that I faced up to the possibility that I might die as a result of this sickness and asked Sue to contact my brother Seymour and older son Adrian. I asked the doctor to delay me going to the operating theatre until my brother came.

When Seymour and Adrian arrived, I burbled something about my will to Seymour and told Adrian that I loved him. I did not have much to say; their presence was enough for me to express all I can say to the people who mean so much to me.

Death, it seemed, had been following me for the last few days. I did not understand; why? If it wanted to take me, why it did not just do so. It was a far more powerful force than my life energies. It could have grabbed me at any moment, but it chose not to. Why?

Was it the prayers that were being prayed for me in the churches and homes across East London? Was God taken aback by the prayers of his devoted followers and had decided to postpone my imminent arrival at the Pearly Gates, whilst he took a deeper look at who was responsible for clogging up the prayer communication lines? Did He, having looked closer at my history on planet Earth, ring up death and say, "Leave this one for now, I will give you someone else in his place. I need to find out why this one is getting so much prayer time"?

And although death agreed to God's wishes, he still skulked, in case I fell over or tripped up, or simply died of exhaustion. Any accident would not be his fault and he could claim me once and for all. And still he stalked and still I evaded him.

He stalked me in the ward, when the doctor injected me with a medicine that seemed to dissolve my entire body and made me feel as if I was effervescing away into nothingness.

He hovered over me when they fitted the catheter between my penis and my bladder and the pain, which seemed eternal, made tears fill my eyes. He was ready to grab me when they gave me the anaesthetics. He sat there ready to spring when they tried to resolve the problem with shock treatments to the heart. After five attempts they gave up and brought me back to the ward.

Death followed me in the ambulance to Bart's Hospital and hid under the bed whilst the heart team first carried out an angiogram, which pushed liquid from the inside of my leg all the way up to my heart to see if there were any blockages in my arteries. Death must have smiled when they fitted the pacemaker to my heart, through my neck. Surely it would get me then.

There is a montage of faces, people, with worried expressions talking to me and looking at the monitor; in fact, what one noticed was that people were not interested in me, just my heart monitor. They cared so much for my welfare that they were looking at the thing that showed them what my heart was doing, rather than at me.

There are memories of long conversations with Sue and Adrian, Seymour, my brother, magnificent in his care, understanding and love. Mum coming in, saying nothing, just looking. Friends from work, some come, look and go away shocked; others stay a long time. Cards and visits from people I had not seen for ages. Well-wishers letting me know how much my life meant to them. Neck covered in blood, friendly nurses, mad cleaners. Breakfast at seven in the morning. Young brother turning up at 8am with cornmeal porridge. Visitors queuing up in the little waiting room. Too many, they take it in turns to come in. Then suddenly it is ten o'clock and Sue needs to go and pick up the kids and I am sad because I will miss her. Adrian goes, Seymour gives me some space and I let Sue know how much I appreciate what she has done and is doing for me. I hope she realised how much she means to me. She goes off and I am alone with my thoughts. I read: three books in two weeks.

But the night comes and I am alone with my thoughts and death. He hides under the bed. He slithers under the door and he makes me know he is waiting for me. One night he comes and he takes someone else and he smiles as he leaves the room. He lets me know that he can take me any time he wants and I am afraid. I am petrified. I half smiled in the night, when the man died, because it was not me. I realised what I was doing and was ashamed.

I was not ready to die. Sure, like all humans, I had bravely stated on numerous occasions that when death comes I would be ready, but I had no experience to base that assessment on. All I had to base my views on was the bravado of life, the feelings of your youth, that you are totally and absolutely invulnerable. These feelings stay with you until you have a major illness that calls into question your security, based on a one heart human model.

I mean how much risk assessment went into that design? It's not exactly designed for long-term viability, is it? Humans cannot live for too long based on the type of vital organs we currently have. Why can't we be like salamanders that can regrow organs if they drop off as they trot their long lives around the world?

I had so much to do. I had always thought I had so much time to do all the things I wanted. I had children to raise, a wife to keep pleasing, the grandchild to shape, and books to write, projects to manage, ambitions to be achieved. I did not have time to die right now and leave all these things behind. What would become of my children and my future, if I was not there to ensure their security? How dare life be so cruel?

And yet life was not all that cruel. For a start, throughout my illness, there had been no internal pain, no pain from within, only the pain that came from the cuts and slices inflicted on me by the doctors in order to save my life. There was blood, but only the amount that had to be spilt in order that I could live. All the pain had come from my fears and the doctors' work. And still death stalked me, joking with me, teasing me, letting me see others die in that cold way he has of making his point.

I eventually made enough of a recovery to be discharged on the 10th December 2000. I came home, determined to make this the best Christmas I had had in ages. There was just so much to catch up on. I was tired, but the time off in a hospital had done me some good, and although my energy level was low, it was high enough for me to do some last-minute shopping for Christmas and get all the presents for the inner and extended family, sort out the itinerary and where we were going for Christmas.

On the 14th December, I got this innocuous letter from Bart's, saying they had been trying to ring me, that when I was discharged, they had forgotten to prescribe amiodarone, the VT control drug they had filled my body with and which was supposed to always be in my body managing the VT. That I should go to my GP immediately and get the prescription. I did not really worry about this, as I was feeling fine. However, I went to the GP, got my prescription and started taking the drug the same day.

Amiodarone is a drug, which slows the nerve impulses in the heart muscle and is used widely to treat abnormal heart rhythms. It is also used to try to prevent recurrent atrial and ventricular fibrillation, and ventricular and supra ventricular tachycardias. The drug is generally reserved for use when other agents have not been effective because it has a number of serious adverse effects, especially when used over the long term. The effects include liver damage, thyroid problems, and damage to the eyes and lungs, and pulmonary fibrosis. Treatment should only be administered under specialist supervision and carefully controlled dosages to optimise results. Not your average paracetamol, I thought. On top of the VT control drug, I was also taking drugs to manage high blood pressure, diuretics to remove excess fluid from my lungs.

My lungs had been damaged when I went into cardiac arrest and then heart failure. Apparently when you die, your lungs tend to get flooded with all the vomit and other rubbish in your body. This makes your lungs very prone to infection after heart failure. I was also taking beta-blockers to slow my heart rate down and oh yes, I almost forgot: they fitted an internal cardiac defibrillator inside me. This, in effect, comes in to play if my heart rate goes above 150 beats per minute. It paces my heart back to normal. If the pacing does not bring the heart rate down then at 190 beats per minute, it delivers a massive electric shock to my heart in an attempt to put it back into rhythm. If, for any reason, my heart should stop, like I am dead, it also provides a massive shock to my heart and will keep on doing so until the battery runs out, whether you are dead or not. It sounds simple and is a magnificent piece of engineering. Cost about thirty thousand pounds fitted.

What the doctors fail to tell you and you do not mention it, because you do not want to sound too ungrateful, is that a man who was a fast bowler in his cricket team, who boxed in the Navy, who saw sport and fitness as a natural extension of his psyche, is going to have psychological problems with something that prevents his arm from being extended too far above the head. This person, who still has not worked out that their life has irrevocably changed and will never be the same again, is going to become bitter sooner or later. And I did.

You see, after you have thanked the Lord, the doctors, your wife, the local MP, the dustman and everyone else for saving your life and keeping you alive, you do start looking at the life you now have and you cannot help being sad and dissatisfied. I could not climb the stairs without running out of breath. I had no strength left in my body; it seemed to have disappeared at the moment of my heart failure, never to return. Even now, I am still not as strong in my body as I was before the cardiac arrest. Then there is the weight loss and the anemic look, the hunted feeling that permeates your very being, the fear that each breath will be your last, which comes from almost every thought you have about everything in the known universe.

Then, when all that has been partly assimilated, you come to the really tricky thing that refuses to be accepted: humans are biological beings. The idea that a bit of metal in your body is all that is keeping you alive makes you feel more robotic and useless than human. As humans, we pride ourselves on our wholesomeness, not the mechanical bits that keep some of us going. If the ICD had been fitted at birth then I would by now have got used to it, its strength and its limitations. At fifty, with a whole lifetime of normal human living behind me, it was hard to accept it as anything but a necessary evil.

It was 5am on Friday, 22nd December 2000, when I woke up with a bit of a start. I felt, from the time my eyes opened and my head cleared, that my old adversary was in the room. Since my stay in the hospital, I always seem to wake up at the same time in the morning. This time, however, it was different. I knew something was seriously wrong. I felt nauseous, faint and out of breath. I automatically checked my wrist and could not believe what was happening. The VT had returned. My heartbeat was up at 140 beats per minute as opposed to the 55 beats per minute it usually ran at.

I went to the toilet and sat down and as I was about to get up, a hand from the netherworld pushed itself up my rectum, grabbed my heart and started pulling it right out of my body. At least that is what I felt was happening. What was really happening was that the ICD had fired its first shock to bring my heart back into its normal rhythm.

The pain was intense. It was not of this world. It was not just painful. It was without any redeeming features in its remorselessness. It just was what it says it was. Absolute pain.

I screamed and in my own head it sounded like the voice of death. I felt that I was dying again, only this time I knew all about it. My first scream woke Sue up. She looked at me, sleep still in her eyes and she must have seen in my eyes what I was feeling because she quickly changed and, even as she was changing, the second electric shock sank into my heart and literally lifted me up from the bedside table, where I was frantically taking my socks and underpants out to prepare for the ambulance I knew would have to take me back to the hospital, and threw me into the middle of the bed. I weighed fourteen stone and I was lifted like a grain of salt and thrown.

I stayed in the middle of the bed, lying foetus-like and minimising my size and dying. And death laughed at me. It said I was a coward who could not take a little pain. It said did I really think I could escape him by going home? Did I not know that he knew where I lived? I lay there foetus-like, trying to get back into my mother's womb, where there would be no pain, where I would be safe.

I lay there and screamed as the third shock came and I heard Sue knocking on our next-door neighbour Simon's door, and Simon, who had already heard the scream and was coming down the stairs as she rang the bell, came over and helped.

I heard Sue's frantic call to the ambulance and their controlled information gathering, which was more than Sue could bear, when the fourth shock slammed into my heart and I screamed again. I glanced at Simon, who was sitting on the stairs, with his head in his hand, looking totally helpless.

I screamed for the fifth, sixth, seventh and eighth shock and wondered whether any God would let anyone suffer so much pain. What, I wondered, was in it for him? I was now waiting for the shocks to come. I thought they would just keep coming until the battery in the ICD ran out or my heart stopped as it had done before. Only this time if it stopped, there was no cardiac crash team to leap to the rescue. There was only Sue, my by now poor hysterical partner, Simon, my next-door neighbour, and my two youngest children, lying fast asleep in their beds, downstairs.

By the ninth shock, I would have welcomed death. I would have gone over to him and said, "It is a fair cop, just take me and let me not have any more pain, and release Sue and Simon from their nightmare. This fight is between you and me, keep them out of it." Only in that dark, stark moment of total and absolute despair, when I looked for him, actually sought him out, death was not there.

Thankfully, the ambulance came just after the ninth shock and I told the paramedics what had happened. They said that I must be having a VT storm, gave me an injection and carted me back to King George's Hospital. I remember saying to the driver that King George's did not know anything about the ICD or VT and it would be safer to take me to Bart's. They said that they could only take me to the nearest Accident and Emergency Hospital, which they then proceeded to do. All the while I was getting apprehensive, as the very place they were taking me was the hospital that had allowed my heart to fail and, as far as I knew, may have compounded the whole problem.

The nurse seemed rather interested in the ECG graphs that had been printed out and they all came to look at the X-rays that showed the ICD fixed in the left-hand side of my chest muscles and all the wires going down to my heart. It seemed and I guessed in the ambulance that I was the first case of a fitted ICD that anyone in the A&E had seen. They did not seem very interested in me and my problem, only in the new technology that was on display inside me. I expected any minute to have interviews with students about my case.

Sue managed to contact Bart's Coronary Care Unit and they told King George's that I was a patient of theirs, and agreed my transfer to Bart's.

I arrived at Bart's at 11.30am and the VT was back in control by 12.30pm. They readjusted the ICD to 100 beats per minute, took control of my heart rhythms and gave me extra doses of amiodarone to speed up the control of the VT. It seems that I could not live without the blessed amiodarone. It was funny: later, much later, the drug would nearly kill me, but right then, it was saving my life, so I welcomed it when they said they had to flood my body with it again to manage the VT.

The consultant cardiologist said to me that a VT storm had occurred, due to the absence of amiodarone in my body for some eight to nine days. They kept me in hospital right over Christmas and Ainsley, Sophie, Sue and I actually spent the day on the ward. I must say that the food was not as bad as I had thought hospital food would be. I was discharged on the 31st December 2000, this time with all my drugs.

I was afraid. It was New Year's night and I was home. For the first few days, neither Sue nor I could sleep in our bedroom. I felt as if an energy source had been left in there from the night of my VT storm. The room's decor was light at the top and dark at the bottom of the room, which gave the appearance at 5am that I was sleeping in a mahogany coffin. I was traumatised.

In my days I could not sleep because I felt that my heart was going to stop at any time and the shocks would come cascading over me again, bringing with them that awesome pain of which I was now petrified. Only this time, knowing my luck, I would be on my own and the ambulance would not come, and so I would die after the ICD had shocked me so many times that the battery would run out.

My nights were filled with the strangest dreams. I dreamt of being chased from one part of the universe to another, by a tireless foe, who was as relentless at chasing me as I was at escaping his clutches. And in the darkness when all around me was still, and only the faint sound of a car can be heard outside your window, you look to make sure it is safe. Your heart beats within the confines of the beta-blocker limitations imposed on it. Your chest heaves, but you do not breathe too hard, as it is painful to do so. And you pray for the next breath.

I twitched when the slightest changes occurred in my breathing. I became obsessed with my pulse. I read it every half an hour or less, only being satisfied if it showed fifteen beats per twenty-five seconds. I would stare off into vacant space, almost waiting for the shock to come and finish me. But it never did. And I said to myself, "This too shall pass", and eventually it did.

I was now on four different tablets per day. One to manage my blood pressure, beta-blocker to control the power and beat of the heart, now enlarged due to the original heart failure, as far as I can gather. On top of these, my lungs, also damaged, needed diuretics to keep them free from liquid. Then there was the amiodarone. For someone who never had time for things like aspirin and paracetamol, the idea of so many drugs going into my body just played havoc with me.

I was out of breath constantly. My body itched incessantly. I was not allowed to go into direct sunlight. I felt faint and dizzy all the time. I did not sleep at nights. Then I developed a dry cough, known in the trade as an ACE inhibitor cough. All due to the side effects and the combination of drugs I was taking.

Sue went back to work in February and I went back in March 2001. I went back to no job (another local authority reorganisation) and an offer of redundancy. That really cheered me up.

Sue and I had a very quiet wedding on the 16th June 2001 at the local register office. It was attended by the youngest of our children and our very best friends who acted as our witnesses. We then went for a meal afterwards. It was simply beautiful.

The doctors decided that I should be medically retired and on the 12th August 2001 I left the local authority for the last time.

Since then, I have been diagnosed as having pulmonary fibrosis, which we believe came from over-exposure to amiodarone. I am on a course of steroids to hopefully reduce the damage to my lungs. My lung capacity has also been restricted, again due to amiodarone. The ICD has not shocked me since December 2000 so I am getting confident in that. Oh and by the way, on the 23rd January 2002 I came off the amiodarone and am now on a less dramatic substitute.

It has taken me sixteen months and a whole raft of changes in my life to get me where I am right now. I am not out of the woods yet. At last I am beginning to think of a new career and what it should be. I have a lot of skills to actively employ. What in or what as, I am not sure yet, but I will be soon.

**I feel that I have been saved for something. I hope it is special. They say that we are just travelling in the slipstream of a rapidly expanding universe, and I once heard a character on *Star Trek* say something like "After the death of life comes the life of death". I don't know if any of those are true. My experiences, however, have made me ready for the transition to the next level, whatever that turns out to be. However, as I look on my children and grandchildren and see them still as templates being worked on by the university called life, I am tempted to say I am ready, but don't take me just yet.**

**Thanks to all those who gave me the opportunity to say to death… not yet.**

# Book 2

# Some Sad, Sad Songs

# The Spark (And Its Afterthoughts)

**Where did you go, where have you been?**
You seem to be lost in the miasma of my uncertainties
If my sudden and untimely death frightened you away
Then please note that I am alive again, so please call
*I need you.*

Without you I am just a list of endless possibilities
An obscured pool of things that could be, but won't be,
Things that should be, but can't be
Without you I am a lifeless cloud of incertitude
An intangible, clarity-free, soulless edifice incapable of actions
Good or bad
*I need you.*

And ah, I remember you so well.
I recall your drive, your ideas, and your get-up-and-go.
You were the tiny grain of energy that ignited my fire
That converted my listlessness into myopic paths of desire
*I need you.*

So many things left me that night, never to return, it seems.
Sometimes I cannot recall how spiritual I was before the journey
I was alive, I woke up alive again, and the middle is gone,
Never to return.
What route did I take? I do not know
Did I stop for a cup of tea? I do not know
I awoke from death, with half of my spirit missing.

Spark, you were just another one of my weapons
That deserted me when the horsemen came calling
Like strength, energy, focus and never say die
You were not there when I woke up.
It seems that you were all too afraid to stay true and loyal.

Or were you all the sacrifice I had to make?
The trade-off made to ensure the certainty of the next breath
The Dane geld paid to be left alone
If so, then you really ought to have asked me
If the next breath was worth such pain, such uncertainty,
**Such intense disillusionment at the mediocrity of what
remains.**

# Afterthoughts

**My soul says to me sometimes that I am a spirit having a human experience and that I should not worry as I will leave all this behind, when I return to my spiritual plane. However, I wonder sometimes whether we are bound to go on and on through these experiences until we find the right solution to the paradoxes they create.**

For instance, if my soul is here to learn how to manage jealousy, then it may go through several divorces and difficult relationships before it finally conceives how to share non-judgmental, honest and pure love based on trust. The pain of those human physical experiences may be such that they create negative spin-offs, which take millennia for my soul to put back into balance.

Oh spark, I miss you.
Maybe you have been carrying me
when I had no other means of support.
Maybe you are the inspiration behind my every waking hour.
Maybe you are there waiting for me to finally realise that you cannot help me until I choose to help myself. Just patiently standing there in the shade, waiting for me to realise that I have been given a new road to travel and that the map has been in my pocket all the time and all I had to do was look for it and it would appear,

**Along with strength, energy, focus and never say die.**

# Managing the Incline

**I am a fifty-eight-years-of-age-old man**
And my mind is not at ease
The messengers are coming in thick and fast
And my destiny cannot be appeased.

We are all born with a billion breaths
And my heart has been beating too fast
And as you know I have not been sitting there counting
So I have no idea how long it is all going to last.

They say it is not the breaths you have
But what you achieve in between
Only sometimes like footprints in a sandstorm
The results can never be seen.

The incline is getting steeper
The blood flows ever so freely now
As I sit here reminiscing
There is something I will avow.

I will not sit there in a wheelchair
Looking out of my window into a brook
Living my last days behind the net curtains
Like some seedy little crook.

I will not be sitting in some wheelchair
Waiting for my next oxygen fix

Blood too tired to move anything
Swallowing my chemical mix.

I cannot sit there in the wheelchair
Waiting for the next cough to slay
All my dreams of a better tomorrow
By stealing my next breath away.

The infections are now on a rota
Ear first and then the chest
Itchy skin, headaches and blood-filled phlegm
To keep me at my best.

It is the little things
Like running upstairs to the loo
It's not major, it's not significant
I mean, it's not like walking to Timbuctoo.

Is it all part of an incline?
In Man's journey from and back to the void
Should I be a little bit more philosophic?
**Instead of so blindingly annoyed.**

# Sharm El Sheik

**An old acquaintance of mine came to visit me in
Sharm El Sheik**
We stopped and exchanged thoughts for a while
I cannot say I was pleased to see him
As he always leaves me with a frenetic smile.

I said I was surprised to see him so far from home
In such a beautiful place
A haven where the sea meets the sky
And blue is the colour of gentle solace.

I normally expect to see him
In a palace of frozen doubts
Or a cauldron of painful memories
Laced with screams and shouts.

I asked if he had travelled so far
Just to idle away some time with me
I explained that I wasn't all that glad to see him
Because of our painful history.

I asked him where his brothers were
As they always seem to travel in fours
He said they were down the road in Palestine
On another of their unending Middle East tours.

Finally I said, why are you here?
You have brought me nothing but pain

All your stories, myths, half-truths and lies
I just could not listen to them again.

He said, sit down and rest your feet
Try and see if you can calm down
I have brought you here to Sharm El Sheik
To replace that age-old frown.

We brothers came to see you ten years ago
And we responded to the prayers to save your life
Finally, I persuaded them to leave you alone
And take that old man and his lonely wife.

I have returned to visit you
To see what you have done with the respite
But all I see is sadness and fear
And a heart that's full of spite.

I see a man so full of pride
A heart becoming stone
Your head was meant to see the stars
But suspicion is all you've grown.

Have you seen the sunset in Sharm El Sheik?
The way the yellow dies and orange calls
The way the orange sacrifices itself, so that brown can live
And then darkness descends on it all.

That is the journey of all that lives
From the beginning to the end of time
And like the sun, my aging son,
You will be taken at your prime.

But... not yet the brothers have told you
Not yet is the plan for you
Just look around and observe the land
And get to know what you can do.

It is ten years since any rain
Has fallen on this barren land
Yet the green shoots of life are everywhere
Like a part of some master plan.

The hot breeze rustles across your skin
And soothes it like a gentle cream
The big red sea, so warm and blue
Just like a little stream.

The sand is in the foreground
It is here, there and everywhere
It defines all that you can do
From here to Timbuctoo.

Despite all its adversity
Sharm El Sheik still wears a smile
No one would ever know it's in pain
Because it carries it all with style.

You do not carry your pain with style
You carry it on your chin
You carry it in your deadened eyes
And in your down-turned grin.

You carry it in your hopeless stare
And in your withered gait
I am beginning to see an absence of hope
And I pray I am not too late.

Take a look at your wife, snorkeling like an innocent child
Seeing, tasting, touching, feeling everything
Almost as if she thinks it's her last day on this planet
And she has to gulp it all in at once.

You were her inspiration
In her dark days, she got reassurance from your smile
She sought solace in your quiet, calm ways
And she has not seen them for a while
All she gets is your angry stare
And you're whining disgruntlement
Constantly,
I mean constantly moaning about everything
And picking those arguments.

She sees things in an uncomplicated way
Life is just to enjoy
Keep it all simple, keep it true
Like a little child with their toy.

But you want to make it all serious
Everything just has to be dark
It must be paranoid and mysterious
Instead of just having a lark.

And in her darkest time of doubt
When she views the road ahead
She wonders if it's worth the ride
With you by her side
Or maybe someone else instead.

Sometimes I glimpse your oldest child
Still searching for his stolen childhood
Still bearing the scars from the pain you gave him
And yet still seeing in you nothing but good.

He is just beginning to turn things around
I can still see the anger in his eyes
When he remembers how you left him on his own
When he was not yet fully formed
You were all he had that could
Have helped him shape his world
Yet you abandoned him half grown.

Your youngest son looks into your eyes
He knows what he is seeking from you
Yet the reassurance he needs, you do not give
Because you are feeling blue
He wants you to be so proud of him

He has achieved it all to make you proud
Now he is getting disenchanted
Getting fed up with your angry stares
And may
One day
Just walk away
Because he no longer cares.

Your daughter has suffered the worst
She has seldom seen the best of you
She can hardly remember
The laughs, the smiles, the silly jokes
And the loving things that fathers do.

All she sees is moody dad
Who never seems to smile
Who constantly points out what she does wrong
But seldom what she does in style.

These are not the reasons we saved your life
Not why you are still here
You have to show us it was worth our while
To keep you living, back there.

You saved my life back there, you sure did
Now I am kept living in a gilded cage
You fill me with steroids and all the other chemical brew
And you still wonder why I am filled with rage.

I was just a simple man
Following a simple plan
Eat to live, not live to eat
Was something simple, even I could understand.

Now you leave me with a body that doesn't quite work
A heart too fat to heave
A lung that cannot generate enough air
For me to bob and weave.

I was born a warrior
Born to act
Not used to living in a frozen chair
Not used to being locked in a panic-looking haze
Because my body cannot generate air.

It's been ten years since you abandoned me here
And each day, I am slowly, unerringly, systematically getting worse
You have taken all my positive surge
And obliterated it with reality's curse.

You expect me to be grateful
I am not quite sure what for
You want my thanks and praises
For an engine that doesn't purr.

They say its seven years of famine, for seven years of plenty
And my famine years now add up to ten
And I wake up happy, expecting to see plenty
But all I get is famine again.

You expect me to be positive
But you have left me armour-less in this fight
Meanwhile the chemical warriors attack me
Leaving me afraid to face another night.

I have sacrificed all my courage
The Dane geld I paid just to stay alive
It was nine times the ICD shocked my heart
Nine times death called and I refused to open the door
Nine times the shock lifted me off the bed
Until I couldn't take any more.

My neighbour sat there, staring in a trance
Scratching his head to keep out the thoughts
Waiting for the ambulance to rescue him
From me and my overwhelming pain.

Your steroids leave me with an ungainly size
Which complicates my gait
The chemo tablets and the other sixteen pills
Make death something I contemplate
The constant flu, the constant colds
From one week to the next
The lack of air
The apoplectic stare
As I fight to suck in my next breath.

And in the stillness of the early morn
When the only voice I hear is the one in my head
When all of my organs are in perfect unison

My rhythms and breaths playing music to my heart
My pacemaker feels like it has also gone to sleep
Leaving my body to play its original part.

I hear a moan of dissatisfaction
Slip-sliding its way into my conscious self
I wonder if I am part of the obvious dream
Coming from the other side of the bed
I wonder what she really thinks
Behind that fulsome smile
How long can she be patient, how long can she be true?
When all she gets is my sullen gloom
And words that are often vile?

And each year I see the small changes
That move things on from the last
Each year I see the colder eyes
That were not there in the past
And I watch in total helplessness
As the cold moves from the eyes down to the mouth
And now those once incessant lips
Just seem to be always closed
The jaws seem to be clenching her teeth
Which widens the flare in her nose.

And early in the morning,
Two strangers lie awake in the bed
Wondering what will become of them
In the coming years ahead

Will she be a very young, but free widow?
Or a bitter, but loyal wife?
Will he find his own salvation, will he come to terms
Or just fade away to oblivion and give his wife a life?

And then I wake and watch helplessly as my family grow
Too tired to play my part
The inability to partake or even share
Just leaves me with a broken heart.

And as I look at Sharm El Sheik
It looks back at me with saddened eyes
It shakes its head in disappointment
When it looks at my demise.

Don't patronise me, Sharm El Sheik,
Sitting there in your monotone brown
While foreigners trample all over you
Because you have forgotten how to even frown.

Your beautiful body is trampled on
By tourists who really don't care
Whether Sharm El Sheik still exists
In another twenty years.

And still you smile your powerless smile
Dreaming of bygone days
When you were the master of the universe
And had skills that still amaze.

The brazen sun rises early in the morning
It leaves no shade in its path
It moves remorselessly across the land
Like a god that's full of wrath.

By midday in the summer months
The sun is a raging cauldron of heat
Even the flies, the roaches and the ants
Have decided to do a full retreat.

And as you gingerly enter into the noonday sun
You feel like a traveller in a barren land
The unearthly beat, the unending heat
As you tiptoe into the water from the sand.

And my acquaintance looked puzzlingly at me
As I gazed trancelike at Sharm El Sheik
He started to reminisce about bygone days
And long gone ways
And some old story about a lake.

I said, listen to me, you impatient old man,
I still have part of my story to tell
Let me explain, what fills me with pain
And when I am finished,
You can drag me down to hell.

Some people live on a positive plane
Leaving others to take the negative strain

They avoid all issues that may cause them grief
While others have to bear them, again and again.

They never see problems, so there is no pain
Life is just like drifting down an easy stream
Flipping from one pleasantry to the next
Eating sweet marshmallows and fondant cream.

In the meantime others are opening the doors
Clearing up the mess left behind by the fondant cream
Fixing the house, making sure the rent gets paid
And making the raft to navigate that stream.

There is very little point explaining how anything works
As nothing can be understood by them, except your
visible futility
And yet they do not do it intentionally
Their ignorance of how the universe works is to blame
They see simplicity and complexity
As one thing and the same.

Life lines have never dared to approach their countenance
The face is as carefree as virgin snow
Meanwhile all round them the supporters are dying
From the strain of producing the daily show.

There is no point seeking reassurance from the void
As it simply cannot understand anyone else's pain
So you just internalise your thoughts
And let the loneliness and solitude remain.

The horseman looked at me with those saddened eyes
That have seen death and rebirth over and over again
He said nothing for a long time
Whilst I managed my wearisome pain
Finally when he saw that I was at ease
He continued with his refrain
Only this time as I gazed into his wizened eyes
I felt compassion for the very first time.

He took my hand and he rubbed the back
As if he was trying to keep me from harm
Only his action in the noonday heat
Made my body feel warm.

Then he said:
You've got to find yourself another voice
With more hope than the one you use
You've got to find another voice
Here are some options from which you can choose
Even in death there is hope
But your voice will not be heard
If in the heat of the battle for survival
You show that you cannot cope.
Be strong, my young survivor,
Show no fear in your heart
Find yourself another voice
And let it play its part.

Let the voice be strong as the rocks on the edge of the shore
Let the voice be as powerful as the wind that blows and blows
Let it be as long lasting as the sand beneath your feet
Let it be as loving as the first suck of your mother's teat
Let it resound, like water from a mighty stream
Let it be as fearless as the warriors in your dreams.
Let it be as loving as the tears that flow from your eyes
Let it be as gentle as slowly escaping sighs

And when you die, the world will know you lived
Because your resonance will still be loud
It will echo all across Sharm El Sheik
It will boom around London town
The gatherings will be enormous
To remember your great deeds
All will have sad, sad eyes,
Reminisce on bygone days
On all that was achieved,
On your life,
Legacy
**Demise.**

# The Lamentations of the Chauffeur, the Taxi Driver and the Submariner

**We sat in the A&E reminiscing about bygone days**
On events from our collective past
On things and times that we all shared
But remembered from a different point of view.

We talked about the Beatles and the Rolling Stones
Fleetwood Mac and Alan Price, Eric Burdon
The Animals and Georgie Fame
Of the Marquee, Ronnie Scott's and Cue
The Rainbow and Whisky A Go Go
That's WAGS to me and you.

The Stones Concert in Hyde Park in Sixty-Nine
The Beatles in Albert Hall
How music is so vital to the young
And reclines as reality starts making the call.

The Chauffeur laughed as he remembered his joyful life
From Bethnal Green to Tenerife
And back to Chigwell
Now he lives quietly in his near resting place
His kids have all done well
He now pays the piper the full fee
For all the scams he's pulled
For all the ruthless misguided decisions he has made
To get himself out of hell.

He lives there in his bloated form
Excesses seeping out of his greasy pores
Heart failure stops him getting fit
And apnea ensures he snores
And yet he laughs in the twilight
As the sun gives up its day
And the moon takes over running things.

He calls himself the Fatman
Yet there is no irony left in his heart
In his eyes there is the resentment
Of life's broken promises about immortality
He thought he would be twenty-five forever
That he would live a thousand years and
Die, still looking and feeling twenty-five.

Now he realises that the parts
Can only regenerate seventy times or so and
Then forever they are gone.
That there is no point living to one hundred and fifty
If your skin has turned to stone
Or worse, simply no longer there.
So we remembered the great days of the sixties
And prepare for the road ahead.

The Taxi Driver laid there in his hospital crib
So small, you thought he was wearing a bib

Lights flashing, sounds alarming
Telling him constantly that he is ill.

He smiles the smile of the fearful one
He puts on his brave face again
And when his heart races to one-six-five
You can see that fearfully remembered pain.

He has been dead four times and brought back to life
He is afraid the next time will be his last
And yet he just keeps going
Long walks his remedy
For battling his long-time enemy
Ventricular Tachycardia.

He tells us about his flashy cars
When he was a king
Driving across America
Just doing his own thing.

He invested wisely and lived very well
Kept driving until he was seventy-five
His heart rate is one-six-two
And he is fast asleep.

He is really fighting old age
Instead of seeing it as his friend
Instead of loving his future
He just wants the change to end.

So he takes on the world to be powerful
Wants to be seen and to be heard
Afraid that his silence makes him invisible
He shouts more loudly now.

And in the quiet of the midnight hour
When he has nothing else to fight
When the certainty of tomorrow becomes clear
When the remorseless energy of old age wins
When the power of his body begins to die
When he knows his memory is gone
When his once golden face becomes ashen
And the hair on his head snowy grey.
When the heart still races at one-six-two
And it's unclear what's causing it all
He blames it on the work he does, the kids,
The stress and the traffic jams
As opposed to his aging frame.

The Submariner sat there observing it all
He was the youngest of the three
He had experienced a multitude of pain
And was worried about it no more
He asked the Chauffeur and the Taxi Driver
Why they were so afraid
They said, of what tomorrow brings
Afraid that there was no certainty
No beginning or end.

The Chauffeur said, the future reveals nothing to me.
You would think after seventy-six years
I would be able to see a lot more
But the older I get, the more uncertain it all seems
Between the memory fade and the energy jade
I have no idea what the next second will bring.

Out of the corner of my eye
A patient is gasping for air
He looks helpless and apologetic
As lack of oxygen makes him stare
The Resus Team rushes over
And Resus him one more time
The man looks relieved, the Resus Team matter-of-factly disband
And we just carry on talking as before.

I said I was a Submariner, joined the Navy in sixty-five
Running away from a pre-arranged destiny
Created by everyone but me.
I did all the things I planned to do
Created a universe of my own
Thought I had everything under control
As if I could do it all alone
Now I have no answers to give
No certainty exists within me
No clarity of thought, just ideas I have bought
That cannot stand close scrutiny.

I have reached the age of the Sage
I thought wisdom would have joined me by now
But all I have are sacks full of questions
**And not one answer I can give.**

# Observing the Death
# of Life and Youth

**Well, I am back in the hospital again**
Observing the death of life and youth
Old age and its cohorts rampaging through the place
Making everything so uncouth.

The racist old man sat in his bedside chair
Refusing all help from anyone who does not look like him
He remembers that all black boys will rob him
He remembers that all Asians live in the garages at the bottom of
gardens
But he cannot remember that he is in a hospital
How cruel is fate.

He shouts that he needs no help
So full of hate, he hates himself.

No visitors come to see him
Dementia has eaten away his smile
Old age has taken away the good memories of his life
And left him with the bile.

Another old man sat there incessantly picking at his bandages
His eyes closed to keep other people's universe out and his own
intact
He picks at every bandage, every label, cannula and all
And smiles when it is all done, because he thinks he is free.

And old age takes no pity on him,
It offers him no hope
When he thinks that's all there is
Prostate Cancer says you forgot about me.

The man in the corner bed sat there observing it all
When I glimpsed a tear coming from his eye
I asked him if it was a tear of sadness or a tear of joy
He said, "I think I just want to die".

I have had prostate cancer and beaten it
My sacrifice for continued life is constant urination
I had throat cancer and beaten it
The Dane geld for that was my mind
I have thrombosis and I manage it
Now I am told I have lung cancer
That chemotherapy may or may not let me live
Old age has finally caught up with me
And I have nothing left to give.

I looked into his face and saw his pain
The death of hope and the oncoming life of death
We get so used to life; we forget that it's a journey
And its final destination is death.

Life is remorseless, it owes you nothing
You cannot win any argument with it
Staying alive always means giving something up.

But remember:
Life can end at birth
Before you are fully formed
Before your mother's breathe has breathed
To make your face feel warm.

Life can end when you are four years old
Mum and Dad just getting used to you
When your footsteps were just getting sure
Life takes a different view.

Life can end at seventeen
As an adult you are just starting out
Sneaking away quietly from Mother's skirt
Before she starts to shout

Life can end at thirty-five
Just when you think you will never die
You will always be there for the wife and kids
So insurance just does not apply.

Life has really been good to us
Has kept us going, long beyond its need
It's not life's fault that man's technology
Is not yet ready to further prolong the seed
So be very careful what you ask for
**Would you really want to live forever?**

# Small Talk about Happiness

**Some say that the height of happiness takes your breath away**
And that the height of ecstasy stops the heart
That sadness also has a role to play
In the grand mosaic called life
But true happiness like gold is not in abundance
With its whereabouts you are sometimes unsure
You have to dig deep to realise it
And its staying power can be a little obscure.

But happiness lifts the human spirit
It's the union of positive hope and joy
The realisation that what was impossible has happened
What was desired and hoped for has become real
What was longed for can now be touched
What was hated and mistrusted can be approached with zeal.

Happiness is the new-born baby looking into her mother's eyes
And she just looking back
Both realising they have an eternal bond
That will never crack.

Happiness is the five year old
Sitting on Daddy's shoulder and seeing all of the world
Feeling the wind rushing past his face
As life begins to unfurl.

Happiness is the sixteen year old
Whose exam answer came just in time

As she was about to hand her paper in
And the answer was sublime.

Happiness is the adventurous young man
Putting his life on the line
Skydiving, boxing, skiing and driving fast cars
Knowing that everything will turn out just fine.

Happiness is the flamboyant cook
Whose recipe worked out a treat
Whose guests could not praise the meal enough
And called it an amazing feat.

Happiness is the nervous dad-to-be
Who has just heard baby's first cry
Who scampers into the delivery room
And is so relieved, he cries.

Happiness is the forty-five year old,
Who has been promoted at last
Just when he was beginning to wonder
If his future was all in the past.

Happiness is the grandparents
Who are now co-joined in the mind
Who walk hand in hand to meet their first grandchild
Knowing the future is secure for their kind.

Happiness is a state of mind
A positive state of being
Where hope and joy come to shape
The universe that you are seeing.

It cannot last forever
Because sadness also has a role in life
But happiness is the absolute release
**That makes it all worthwhile.**

# Job's Harvest

**Somewhere, out there, in a world so harsh**
An aging man wept a tear
He'd been working hard, toiling the land
Solidly for a year.

There was nothing to show, nothing to see
For all the hard work he had done
The seeds were still lifeless in their pods
Like there was no rain, or rising sun.

How would he feed his children?
What would the family do?
The ground just sat there looking lifeless
And hopelessness was all that grew.

On harvest morning, he sat in his fields
Quietly, observing the land
Seeing barren fields where life should be
And trying to understand.

"My God, why hast thou forsaken me?
What have I done wrong?
Have I not been worshipping you?
Did you not hear my prayers and songs?

"You say you are the mighty one
You can do miracles, in your sleep
You say you made the universe in six days
And yet, you just watch us weep.

"You said you would always be there for me
To protect me in times of strife
You know what was, what is and what will be
Yet you starve my children and wife.

"We cannot live a year without food
My family will surely die
Yet your power could have saved me
So, why? My Dear Lord, why?

"How could you fail to help me?
Why give me so much pain?
How, and when, did I offend you so much?
**My Dear Lord, please explain"**

I need not explain anything to you
How dare you question my plan!
Do you think that you can anticipate me?
I was here before the void began.

You offer me your songs and praises
Wanting mighty miracles in return
Then the rest of the week you deny and shun me
And expect me not to feel spurned.

Where were you when I built Alpha Centauri?
Do you know why my insects have lived so long?
Have you seen the view?
From the sixth moon of the Globus Nebulae?
Or the beings who live in the diamond rocks of Patong?
Do you think what you see is all there is?
Some things are worth more than your praises and songs.

If you truly believed in me
There'd be no hopelessness in your mind
I do know what was and what will be
And I can save the future from behind.

So, go away and weep no more
The future is what I decide it to be
There will be another tomorrow
As long as I decide it will be.

## Tell Me... Sweet Lord

Tell Me... Sweet Lord
Why You Turn Your Back On Me?
Tell Me... Sweet Lord
Will It Be For Eternity?
Tell Me, Tell Me, Sweet Lord, Just
Tell Me Till I Understand
Tell Me... Sweet Lord
Is This Part Of Your Master Plan?

Tell Me... Sweet Lord
Tell Me What I've Done Wrong
Tell Me, Tell Me, Sweet Lord
Why Redemption Is Taking So Long?
Tell Me, Tell Me, Sweet Lord, Just
Give Me a Little Sign
Tell Me... Sweet Lord
Is This Pain Something Divine?

Tell Me... Sweet Lord
How Long This Has Got To Last?
Tell Me... Sweet Lord
How Long I Have Got To Fast?
Tell Me, Tell Me, Sweet Lord, Just
Tell Me Till I Understand
Tell Me... Sweet Lord
**That It Is Part of Your Master Plan.**

# There Is No Pain

**There is no pain, there is no pain**
But the red river flows deeply outside my veins
The crustaceous pulmonary fibroids open to create a pathway
The chemical dam weakens and gives up in vain
But there is no pain, there is no pain

There is no pain, there is no pain
Not intense pain
Not the pain from an ablated heart
That leaves you just wanting to die
The stomach cramp holds you in its grip
The fingers refuse to bend and stay stiffened like I have no joints
But there is no pain, there is no pain

And in the far distance the sound of winter, like a remorseless ex-
press train,
Whistles its intention to end the summer reign
And it tells you it is on its way.
The coughs are surlier now, not so easy to fob off.
They stick to the inner membranes and need more muscular en-
ergy to bring them up.

The breath runs out of vigor and refuses to return.
It just hangs there, like an unfinished question.
And in the ensuing battle, between my lungs and my heart,
The red river flows deeply outside my veins.
And my body, accustomed to the sounds and what they bring,
Becomes anxious in the impending anticipation of doom.
**But there is no pain, there is no pain**

# Reflections and Final Words

A nd I questioned the Lord. Like Job, I too asked him why. Why the long unremitting road of pain and uncertainties? Why has the gloom stayed for so long? I have carried these uncertainties and reducing quality of life for the last fourteen years.

Fourteen years of wondering whether this breath is my last. Whether the heart can stand the 220 beats per minute that plagues it now and again. The eighteen tablets and their side effects, which keep me bloated, seized with chest cramps, urinating constantly, out of breath and generally sad most of the time.

The nineteen shocks that the ICD has given me in those fourteen years. The twenty procedures including three replacement Internal Cardiac Defibrillators, five angiograms, two ablations to remove the ventricular tachycardia, the chemotherapy-based day-long drips to stop the pulmonary fibrosis from spreading even further, the Lung Function tests, which just leave you wanting to die, when you have no breath to breathe.

The enlarged heart, which is now only forty percent efficient, the pulmonary fibrosis-ridden lungs working at thirty-six percent capacity, the reduced ability to withstand infections and the osteoporosis, the constant blood tests, the constant uncertainties. The psychological pressure of knowing that you are chronically ill and can die any minute.

Then there is the sleep apnea, which started when I was on 40mg of steroids daily and my weight increased to the point of making me look deformed. So now I wear a CPAP mask to bed and still I do not sleep and am sometimes too tired to think.

There has been a tremendous cost to all of my relationships. I have not been a great patient. I think I would have given up without the anger and frustration to spur me on. But these things have an effect on my children, my wife and other people who care for me and I for them.

In my moments of desperation and impatience, I forget that they cannot understand what it is like for me and I cannot understand what it is like for them. It is like we are travelling in the slipstreams of entirely different universes.

I retired a few months ago from working three days per week. The walk from the car park was becoming too much and I was in danger of becoming the office joke when I fell asleep at my desk or in meetings. I, the once so proud military man, was becoming an embarrassment to myself.

It is early November 2014 and the hospital has told me that I need to have another ablation to remove the new tachycardia pathway in my heart and that I may need to replace the ICD for a more sophisticated model. All this needs to be done fairly soon.

I am also being actively encouraged to start taking Warfarin, which I am resisting strenuously, as I think that with this level of medical complications, it would be almost impossible for me to mentally process another complex routine. Just too many issues to think through.

It is fourteen years since my heart failed and still I am here. Still I am hopeful that tomorrow will find me here. Still I pray that a positive outcome is around the corner. I keep saying to myself, THIS TOO SHALL PASS, and maybe tomorrow, it will.

**And although reality keeps hitting me relentlessly, still I live in HOPE, not hopelessness.**

Roy Merchant

November 2014

Printed in Great Britain
by Amazon.co.uk, Ltd.,
Marston Gate.